C0-DBS-104

The Pleasures of C

811.54
Sm18

The Pleasures of C

—

Edward Smallfield

LIBRARY ST. MARY'S COLLEGE

WITHDRAWN

Apogee Press
Berkeley · California
2001

Some of these poems have appeared in the following periodicals:

Barnabe Mountain Review: "Blue Room," "Paris"
Battery Review: "Divinations," "Woman Speaking, Street Corner"
Caliban: "Stain"
Coracle: "Crepuscule with Nellie," "In Weston's Portrait of Tina,"
    "The White Iris"
Fourteen Hills: "Postcards"
Manoa: "The Interpretation of Dreams," "Our Small Republic," "Prostate,"
    "Secret Lives"
The Montserrat Review: "Pannonica"
Painted Hills Review: "February 14, 1994," "Firenze," "Running"
Santa Clara Review: "A Simple Metaphor," "Chapter 27," "John Coltrane,
    Half Note, 1960," "Seventh Age"
Seven Hundred Kisses: "Geography"
Transfer: "Amazing Grace"

Book design by Philip Krayna Design, Berkeley CA.

Cover photograph, "Nude Floating, 1939," by Edward Weston.
©1981 Center for Creative Photography, Arizona Board of Regents.

©2001 by Edward Smallfield.

ISBN 0-96699-376-4. Library of Congress Catalog Card Number 2001-129069.

Published by Apogee Press, Post Office Box 8177, Berkeley CA, 94707-8177.

for vc
"the secret hero of these poems"

Table of Contents

–I–

Crepuscule with Nellie

If this twilight
mumbles a little,
if a few
French vowels
sneak into the glare
as it retreats
over the river,
that's because the hand
stroking this piano
also holds her hand
all the way to Hackensack.

Two minutes
forty-nine seconds
of dusk
whenever you listen.

A few small mammals
escape from the museum.
This buck
four inches high
with enormous antlers
carved
three thousand years ago
from obsidian
skitters now
across six lanes of traffic
to browse a few maples
flagrant beside the river.

Woman Speaking, Street Corner

swollen and pointillist
these lights

a little jazz piano
if you could see the notes
acrobatic and flushed

one earring glitters

in this hour
of erasure

she belts out

hear her warning
or threat

as a blues singer might

or that other
woman
simply walking

against the headlights

Live at the Five Spot

somebody's wife
holds a tape recorder
at the bottom of an elevator shaft

a few notes seep through

nobody remembers who plays bass

Coltrane blows in

fired from one job
about to be fired again

ice cubes
somebody lights a cigarette

Monk follows

a staircase
ascends
into silence

not the notes you play

grabs Rimbaud's small hand
in his enormous grip
full of rings and cigarettes

the notes you don't play

somewhere between
Harar and Charleville

they step off the boat

we've come this far
to learn drowning

A Simple Metaphor

last night's moon

about half
and the enormous bulk
of the acacia

already in August
dark comes sooner

a neighbor makes love

her shrill
repeated note

sign of an edge
she finds
then lingers on
finally passes over

somewhere a piano

a little dirt
clings to each note

this phrase
throbs then stammers

aching
three times
four

these fingers
annotate the night

Pannonica

Parker died on her couch
bleeding ulcer
no hospital

between fifty and sixty
a doctor wrote
on the death certificate
reading his thirty-four year old face

Monk plays her now

some kind of baronness

her accent half Dietrich
half Lotte Lenya
a little Jeanne Moreau around the mouth

a communist with gold coins in her underwear

sometimes Monk tells this story
about her father

I don't think
he ever caught
that butterfly

enormous syllables
never spoken on this planet

a saxophone whispers
blue neon
across her skin

John Coltrane, Half Note, 1960

Without his horn.

Framed by a dark
doorway or window,
right hand a blur

of glare
          as he leans back
on his arm—

a big man's relaxed posture.

That he should know his strength,
the weight
          of the body
he rents in these years.

His left hand rests against his lips

as if he might succumb
to a sudden need
for solace
          and suck
his own skin.

On a hanger
a white coat waits
for somebody who needs
thin cloth
          against this cold.

Just as a singer
lingers, all night sometimes,
until a song arrives.

Round Lights

the shape of his notes
an angular ellipse

between coal
and diamond
he fondles this

lips parted
about to speak
or sing

some kind of standard

around his head
the lens arranges
tentative haloes

no words

except the tune
he fingers

–II–

Divinations

Rosary

What grows on small bushes, rags of color and scent. Or lists of those. Hanging around your neck. A list you make with your breath. Repetition. Incantation. Language dissolved in music. You walk naked in your beads, crossing a street in your big white hat. A foreign language. Words neither of us knows. All those old men, kneeling, hats in hands, after they've peed in the bushes.

Wrench

What you hold with, before you verb. As in—shoulder from the. Leverage. A long handle. That long spoon you sup the devil with. Give me a lever long enough. That tension in. How the torso torsos. Sweat a little. Let that wetness drip. Wipe the salt away. Step closer to your little furnace. If you were the devil, I'd feed you with my fingers.

Scar

Nub of. Re-knit. Harder, stronger, where the hurt was. Raised and pale—what the finger finds, the tongue. Residue, memory, snapshot. Who did it, and why? That window, hook, bat, fist. A fall. An accident. That other word. The white one. A coin you pick up on the sidewalk. You bathe mine with your mouth, and I'll bathe yours with mine.

Compass

That circle we contrive to be inside, or outside, of. Or the needle within, wavering. That you should march north, past the tree line, across granite, until the water is too cold to drink. Lost in the woods. Without one. To make a fire. By rubbing together. Donne's dance of separation and junction. A boundary. That instrument you fiction your edge with. That is: your mouth.

Algebra

From the Arabic. Reunion of. Broken parts. Positive, negative. That the signs should fit. Or not. A transposition. If x equals. Shall you be x, or shall I? Mr. White, Mr. Pink, Mr. Blue. Ms. Brown. Mrs. Black. The molecules that grab each other, and the molecules that don't. A textbook or treatise. You read mine while I read yours.

Alignment

What the car wheels are out of. Because somebody banged the curb. Always you, or your mother. Never your father. A man at the garage hoists the car on a rack and does it with a machine. Or is that balancing? No, balancing is little weights, and Vermeer's girl in a blue smock holding her delicate contraption. This is greasy, muscular, sweaty. Also, your planets—Venus, Mercury, Jupiter, Mars—all in a line. Billiard balls. Pick up the cue, and stroke. A little chalk, first, for delay. As in music, poetry, or fucking. Our alignments never *mal*, our asters never *dis*. It's just a word I found in your dictionary.

Dictionary

Every poet needs a big one. Preferably blue. The blues, blue
Monday. Also, blue movies, blue jokes. Or red. Not *stop*, the red
rag that makes the bull *go*. Enrage me. Word me, breathe me.
Yours, when you open the cover, is entirely blank. Of course.
A poet wears her words in her head, speech she sucked with
her mother's milk. After midnight, your pen scars the *blancs*.
Less beautiful, maybe, but more eloquent. Yours is too heavy
to lift, anyway. Diction. *Dictio*. Speak.

Mass

The measure of inertia in a body. The old priest mumbles, incom-
prehensible, in Latin or English, behind his brogue and the
morning's wine. *As indicated by the acceleration imparted.* A scent
of incense stains the church. *Imparted to it when acted upon.*
Frankincense, probably, what the wise men brought. *By a given
force, which may be expressed.* When the boy drags the surplice
on, that scent clings. *As the quotient of the weight of the body.* As a
lover's scent adheres in later life. *Divided.* How the definition of
holiness changes over time. *By acceleration due to gravity.*
A force you can't resist, gravity—the old man couldn't keep his
hands off the boys. *In painting, the solid, unified portions of color
or light in a composition.* A little town, the last stop for molesters
and drunks. *In pharmacy, the thick, paste-like combination of drugs
used for making pills.* Those were the hands that elevated the
host. *The great body or majority of ordinary people.* Who cares
who does the magic? *A musical setting of fixed portions.* High,
low. *A celebration of that liturgy.* Critical.

–III–

Blue Room

Sitting on the bed's edge, a woman adjusts her stockings.

A little of her garter belt shows, the kind your mother wore, years before pantyhose.

Through the window a streetlight drops its glow on a deserted sidewalk.

In the drawer of the nightstand, a Gideon Bible.

When you enter the room, she looks up, eyes a little paler than her dress.

Blue air. Blue music floats through the window.

Later, while you walk, headlights probe her face. In a small restaurant you eat oysters.

A pile of oyster shells. What Tranströmer calls *experience, beautiful slag.*

At midnight she wakes, turns on the lamp, opens her Bible.

As she reads her lips move, careful with each syllable.

Words the color of crows. Flying, one by one, into the light.

Prostate

An eel in a Swedish poem: *white, frighteningly big, blind, coiling in and out of the riddles of its body...* That's a fairly accurate picture of the gland I imagine.

A secret. At work inside the body. A woman in an attic who writes, then locks the pages in a drawer.

A worker whose business is pleasure. The manufacture of desire.

Stroked by sound, the prostate shines. A song, the notes too high to hear, projects shadows on a screen. The center of attention, a star irradiated by flashbulbs.

I lie with my face to the wall. A boy who pretends to sleep, so his parents won't know that he hears what is happening.

Hey, Dr. V, the woman who takes the picture yells into the hallway, *you wanna look at a prostate?*

A partly muscular gland at the base of the bladder and surrounding the urethra in male mammals, providing some of the chemicals necessary for the production of sperm.

As a man grows older the prostate stiffens. Loses elasticity. Enlarges. Presses the bladder, creates a boyish urge to pee constantly. Becomes cancerous, spreads throughout the body.

A metaphor for desire. What we use, what we don't use. What uses us.

The doctor and nurse study the pictures. The star revealed in her many poses. Lateral, dorsal, transverse. Prostrate. So bare the glare hurts. Not naked, but stripped, peeled.

Written in secret. Locked in a drawer. The urge to speak what isn't spoken.

Stain

After midnight my uncles skin the season's last buck. A small deer, maybe a hundred pounds, gutted, his slender antlers barely legal.

From our attic we can see everything. Blood in puddles, knives.

Because we've seen everything, we believe nothing. Certainly not these old men, too feeble to peel the dead animal.

My grandfather, who's been dead for twenty-five years, drags his thumbnail across the deer's belly, from the base of the throat all the way to the balls. Then he jerks the skin away in one piece, tosses the bloody hide in a corner.

My father hovers at the light's edge. If you ask him tomorrow, he'll tell you he was somewhere else, a little boy who won't admit he watched this striptease.

You want to steal the deer's hide, wrap the bloody fur around your skin and dance.

The deer has been dismantled. Scattered on the garage floor, the pieces remind us of a clock dissected by a child. A puzzle nobody can put together again. You recall your anatomy textbook, name the lungs and heart for me, the gall bladder, kidneys, and spleen.

I read a passage translated from my mother's mother's language. *Male and female witches arrived on the backs of animals or transformed into animals themselves.*

Just look away, you tell me, and the whole scene disappears. I close my eyes, and the world shrinks to the size of my body. I feel your breath against my face, wet patches where our bodies touch.

My father takes his shirt off. I don't want to look at his skin, so pale it seems somehow feminine.

An odor hangs in the air. A blood scent, the memory of the deer. Or seawater, a residue of the chemistry of your body against mine.

I shiver, my teeth chatter. My father wraps his shirt around my shoulders.

Secret Lives

An author writes of his father's life. In a vast house the old man inhabits a single room. Each day he chooses the same suit from his full closets. He seems a photograph of himself, unchanging as his business crumbles around him. Younger women appear with him in snapshots. After the old man's heart attack, the son discovers a supply of condoms. I abandon the book, still open, on a table in the library.

At dinner with a couple I don't know, friends of my wife, I hear a curious story. The man, about my age, explains that his father led a double life. Two wives, two sets of children. He speaks of his recent efforts, long after his father's death, to locate the members of that other family. When he found a half-sister, he couldn't understand her reluctance to meet with him. She was dying of cancer. What, he asks, did she have to lose? Finally she agreed to see him. The man does not describe that meeting. As he speaks it becomes clear that he was a member of his father's second family, a character in his father's secret life.

That night I can't sleep. I remember my father's hands, so big that his coffee cup always seemed about to break. In spite of his strength, my father remains insubstantial. Sometimes I wonder if he hired an actor to portray him. Especially after my mother died, when I felt that his real life must be elsewhere. With his friends at work, or with a woman he had to keep secret for

some reason I couldn't understand. An actor's most difficult-
role must be to establish his character on an empty stage. Light
seeps through the curtains, a stain on the darkness in which I've
failed to sleep. I can't bear the thought that my father may have
had no secret life.

Paris

There is, mother, a place in the world called Paris.

Aprés le dejeuner, au café, my mother lights a Gauloise, flicks some ash onto her plate, blows a cloud of bluish smoke into my face. I start to lecture her about smoking, then remember she's been dead for thirty-two years. The obvious signs of age in my face don't trouble her. Maybe she forgets that I'm her son—I see that neither my father nor my wife is here to remind her. Always talkative, she's almost giddy as she babbles about movies—*Bob le Flambeur, Tirez sur le Pianiste, Le Souffle au Coeur, Les Enfants du Paradis*—that I know she never saw while she was alive. As she speaks I notice her resemblance to my youngest daughter, especially her sea green eyes and the great bush of auburn hair she still wears fifties style, in a permanent wave. She reminds me that Vallejo learned to walk in a special way so that his shoes wouldn't wear out. As she recites his poem about chestnut trees I look out the window and see chestnuts in full leaf, green at midnight where streetlights caress the tips. Through our window a few barges remember the Seine's current. *Let's step on one of those boats,* my mother says, *and ride to Dijon. Then we'll take a train to the Saône and flow to the sea, float the Mediterranean to Africa and disappear.*

–IV–

Luna Mexicana

Eighty miles per hour.
Tumbleweeds scrape the car,

boney halos,
bodies without body,
these long dead souls alight

to scratch the door
of a rusty Volkswagen.

My wife and daughter doze
while I pee
into this endless book of sand.

Moon
a peso,

dirty silver,
slut for a thousand hands,
bright enough to drive by.

Borrowed radiance
chars my shadow.

A stain
on blond dust. Nickels
linger in my pocket,

unspent. Erased by wind
and rain my residue

dissolves
in noon's reshuffled pages,
night's salt.

Amazing Grace

A few words
        from the hymn
as I first heard it, in 1964,
arrested, after so much
church Latin, by the vulgate
pouring from the marchers' mouths.

October sun. Almost children,
in a game, sitting
around a police car.
The scene
        drenched in song

someone who unfolds
a letter, not to read it,
but to see the shape
of that handwriting again

the whole machine stalled in that moment.

Firenze

Gridlock in the Piazza
SS. Annunziata, rain
like cold spaghetti water
through a colander. At the hotel
Colleen folded her small body, snored
through her cold while we fumbled
together in bed, then dozed.
I want to reach back
for some moment, maybe
the view from the Duomo, light
pouring over us until we feel
alive inside a halo.
All I get is that first
afternoon, dingy rain, then
the next morning, patched
clouds and sun when I start
for the park with Colleen
we go through the Via
della Colonna to the Accademia to look
at the slaves' torsos caught
emerging from marble, my favorite
with his head still lost
entirely in stone.

Running
for Eve

Out there, in the deep grass, wildflowers flare
on their wiry stems. I wish I knew their names,
common and Latin. Then I could bore you
properly, then I could chant pure information,
stuff you don't want to hear, but will care about,
when you're my age, and have forgotten
everything. Keep running. If I don't
keep running, I tell myself, I'll petrify,
become a man in a story who ends up
pointing to where the old road used to be.
So we move together through this dust,
through the weedy California August. Let me catch
my breath, if you let me breathe we can run
forever, if you want, past the fence
into the grass, stopping now and then
to pick the stickers from our socks.
After the hills give up and lie flat
the grass around us won't be grass,
but a cash crop, maybe alfalfa, thick
and green, the odor intoxicating,
as we move more slowly, pausing
to drink from garden hoses
behind farm houses in the valley.
Then we can hitch a ride across
the Sierras and western Nevada, halfway
to the salt flats. Wyoming,
Nebraska, Highway 80

just as direct and bleak as it was
when I drove west, not east, when you
were two and I was still married
to your mother. Maybe in upstate
New York we can stop in front
of a hospital and stare at the lights
of the maternity ward as I did
fifteen years ago, and at the Atlantic
edge we'll head south toward Tierra
del Fuego or maybe we'll just keep walking
across the waves. Right now, though, nails
and gravel rattle in my left knee and you
have geometry homework due tomorrow
and a basketball game on Saturday.
So we turn at the gate, limping back
along the same dusty track, abandoning
this language that isn't
our bodies breathing hard right here
where you are the one
who must keep running
long after I'm through.

February 14, 1994

for Kathleen

So much marsh, you can't see
where it ends—that's what
I'd give you, the light
a little patchy, smudged by mist
as if somebody wants to erase
all this, and fails, while the birds
rise—herons, egrets, grebes—
yes, I've learned the names
from you, but not the shapes,
to me those shadows are just
shadows, stringy meat
that must taste of clams
and the oil our tankers spill,
and for the pleasure
of hearing I ask for more names—
loons, buffleheads, mergansers—
and as you speak I see
you sweat in the winter sun
after so much walking, your wet
skin shares the chemistry
of this marsh, iodine and salt,
as if the water were our bodies
turned inside out, and you look
west, toward the Farallones,
where giant sponges swell
on nuclear waste—

avocet, you say, widgeon, coot,
godwit, bittern, stilt, plover—
I wonder when you'll come
to the end and if
you'll begin again,
though by now the sun
sits on the water
and in that glare you can't see
where it ends, this marsh
I'd give you, if the water
wasn't here already, and you
inside its salty light.

Fireworks over Ryōgken Bridge

Poetry is a human art,
like cocksucking, like finding
the angular knees of young men
under after midnight tables at Brink's
or the Blackstone Grill. Always
fireworks: under a sky
of dark blue gin
Hiroshige has filled the harbor
with boats. You see
I've learned to do this
just like you—one visual
reference, one dropped name,
a couple of autobiographical
details. Always
in italics, those quotes—
a man cannot be a poet
if he died. Hiroshige's
capillary of fire ascends,
apogees and wilts, a dazzling
plummet earthward—
because all desire dissolves
in gin, in night, in sleep,
in dreams, in poems. So many boats
under that bridge, and on one
a man's hand finds a man's knee
under an after midnight table.
What did you say in those hours?
Your alchemy can change my clay to skin.
By our human art, we mime the sleeper till we dream.

–V–

The Interpretation of Dreams

A desk, so big and black and shiny that it reminds me of a coffin. If I touch it, I'll leave fingerprints, and they'll know I've been here. I open the top drawer anyway, and find piano keys inside. The keys are connected to wires hidden in the desk. If I touch them, I'll hear music. I listen to the silence inside the room. No cars in the street, no voices in the hall. I bang my fist against the keys, and a ribbon of music unrolls inside my head. I recognize it—something from the Goldberg Variations, one of the faster pieces, elegant, but somehow frayed, as if the notes are beginning to unravel. Then the music stops. I look around the room, and nothing has changed. By the bookshelf I find a large couch and stretch out on it. From this vantage point I recognize the room. This is the Oval Office. After the President has made a particularly painful decision, he invites his secretary into the room, and they make love on this couch. Enormously comfortable, it resembles the couch in my psychiatrist's office. The black leather reminds me of a gondola sliding through the watery streets of Venice. My psychiatrist wears a black leather jacket, approximately the same color as the couch, and above his desk he keeps a medieval map of Europe. At the edges, where the geographer's knowledge fades, dragons blow fiery breath. I see a similar map on the wall of this room. The President often gets up from his desk and walks to the wall to study the map. Now the phone on the desk rings. I pick it up, no longer worried about fingerprints. You're on the line, calling from Yeltsin's office in the Kremlin. You speak Russian, a language neither of us knows, and I understand you perfectly.

Peasants, kulaks, lumpen proletarians—all of them are massing outside the Winter Palace, while the army slips quietly into position around them. When I ask you what year it is, you tell me it's summer. Thrushes chatter in the birches, and the sun burns at midnight while the river flows green to the sea. What, I ask, can I do to help you? Nothing, you say, it's over, finished, complete, done. Some last Russian word comes through the line, untranslated, more final than anything I've heard in English yet. Don't stop talking, I beg you, tell me more. There's light, you say, spilled on everything, drenching the sky, drenching my skin, so much light my eyes can't take in any more, so much light that my eyes read it as darkness.

How the Late October Novel Begins

The scent of the forest floor, mushroom and pine and decay—
that's how the dream ends, after the woman's body stops
squirming, whether in pleasure or pain he can't tell. As he lies
in bed, half-awake, the dream fades, and the smell of death in
the house assaults him. You haven't decided yet whose death
should obsess him. Probably you'll choose his father, though
that seems somehow wrong, a deflection of your mother's
death when you were about the character's age. Perhaps your
whole approach is too oblique. Even the title has been stolen,
but also incorrectly translated, misremembered. At least the
young man's teacher is clear in your mind. A heavy woman,
fleshy and pale, she flushes when she lectures. While she speaks
the class ignores her. Only your character listens, and he can't
understand what she means. She lectures on the brain, so that
you'll have to buy a biology book, learn the names of the lobes,
what each one does. Today she digresses, as she so often does,
and discusses the alchemy of scents. Of course she fascinates
the young man. He wants to tell her about the smell of death
in his house, the scent of the forest floor in his dreams. You'll
have to repeat the dreams, creating a kind of counterpoint,
gradually revealing their content. You must hint at a subtext
inside him, a dark inner life that he doesn't understand. You
must also work in the crimes, a series of rapes and murders
that haunt the inhabitants of the town. Your protagonist feels
linked to those crimes by his dreams, but he can't admit that to
himself. Of course you won't provide all the details—you don't

want to write pulp fiction—but you must hint at sinister particulars you won't reveal until later, if at all. Will you allow the reader to believe that the young man may be implicated in those crimes, not just in his own mind, but in reality as well? You remember the fragment whose title you've stolen, how the boat's motor throbs at the center of the prose, a metaphor so insistent that your head aches as you read. Maybe you should have begun as that other author did, or maybe you shouldn't have begun at all. You try to imagine the young man in his bed as he wakes from the dream you find so disturbing. But he insists on standing at his teacher's desk, after her lecture, waiting to speak to her. Her perfume, mingled with the scent of her body, reminds him of something.

Seventh Age

From this window, night forms a seamless block of tar, but he doesn't need light to see the garden. The tulips have already flared and faded. He insisted on them over the gardener's objections. Now there are only variations on purple and green, lavender and those native plants whose names he's never bothered to learn. *You're a writer*, a friend tells him, *you ought to know the names of your own plants*. A blue flower, a tiny bell, bloomed briefly in the old country every spring. How harsh that name would sound here, a hiss like hot iron against flesh. He has gotten up to pee. Standing over the toilet, he squeezes out a few drops. No pain, just the unrelieved urge to urinate. Like a little boy, he thinks, feeling that he's going to pee in his pants. He stares into the blank wall of night. I should fire the gardener, he thinks, and surrender to the weeds. Seeds would drift across the fence from his abandoned yard. But he won't give his garden to the weeds. He has always been a careful man. When he remembers his second lover, an older woman, he wonders how much more often he could have had her if he hadn't been afraid of her husband. In those days, just after the bombing had stopped, a human life was worth a few coins, the quick flicker of orgasm. An older woman, his first real lover. Now he realizes that she was little more than a child. Afternoons with this woman expand as slowly as oil poured from a bottle. She makes love with her mouth, with her anus. After love, he stands at a window, looking through pearly drizzle at a shattered city. She sits at the mirror, dabs a little scent on her throat, her armpits and breasts. He remembers the line, *The soul is a woman, fond of trifles*, then watches, fascinated, as she paints her mouth. The red stick darkens the lips his lips have bruised, remakes the mouth his mouth erased.

Our Small Republic

On Saturday afternoons a wind blows from the west, off the water. An old man shivers inside his coat and sucks at his cigarette as he waits to buy his ticket for the matinee. Because we still allow smoking in our theater, the tips of cigarettes glow in the darkness, ephemeral as fireflies. From our balcony we watch as the old man buys his ticket, then shuffles into the theater. *Le Notte di Cabiria* plays today, as it does every Saturday. Because he sees the film every week, the old man knows the screenplay by heart. He repeats whole scenes, at the café, when he's drunk enough, in Italian, though he doesn't understand that language. Maybe after we make love we'll get up and watch a few minutes of the film. We might catch the scene with the fortune teller, or the one in which the young man steals Cabiria's money but can't bring himself to throw her over the cliff. She walks down the road, in despair, crying, and the carnival music starts and the bicycles pass and she smiles. Maybe we won't get up for the movie at all. Maybe we'll just lie in bed, as we so often do on Saturday afternoons, dozing and making love again, waking entirely only when the kids march down the street, singing our anthem, on the way back from the park. Maybe then we'll stroll to the beach. We walk for a while, wading out as the tide recedes. You name the soft creatures in those pools for me, and I forget the names as fast as you utter them. We step inside one of those concrete bunkers left over from the last war, the one nobody remembers any more. The bunker smells of seawater, and of the lovers who huddle there, shuddering together. Back in town, we stop at the café. We pause outside, studying our local vulture as it wheels over us, wings reduced by distance to a letter from an unfamiliar alphabet. The old man is inside, working on his first *vin rouge* and describing the film. He's delighted, surprised, as though he's just seen it for the first time. We settle at a table with our coffees, listening as the old man plays each scene word for word, gesture for gesture—Cabiria in despair, Cabiria in love, Cabiria laughing. As we listen we wait for the kids to return. Tonight they're a little late, those kids with their song, and their rope, the rope they tie around the doorknob of the café. Then they pull, slowly, with patience, with the strength and persistence of children, pulling until the town comes loose from its moorings, and the café and the movie theater and our balcony slide downhill toward the sea, across the sand into the water. They sing as they drag us under the waves, burying our republic in the depths of the sea, as they do every Saturday.

Geography

Purple flowers. Wide as trumpets, so delicate they wither in my fingers. Where are you? On the balcony, I suppose, watching as the crowd from the ferry disappears in the streets above the harbor. Sun works on your face, a careful pencil, perfecting your skin. Later, when I touch your cheek, I feel sun concealed inside you. I close my eyes, see those flowers again. When I touch one, I find a membrane, sensitive as the inside of your mouth. While we make love, a little light trickles around the curtain. A wind knocks our shirts from the balcony. After we finish, we walk downstairs to pick them up. Because it's so late, we don't bother to dress. Your red shirt and my white one shine under the streetlight. When a car stops, and the driver asks us why we're naked, we tell him we're dead people who've returned to gather lost garments. He believes us because he doesn't speak our language. Then we slip into his cab and you promise him a coin he's never seen before. *Where,* he asks, *is your asphodel?* so we try to pick some in the field beside the road. We can't find asphodel, so we choose fennel, flagrant at this time of year. We drive all night, in circles, around the island. When we stop in a small store for beer, or in a restaurant to eat lamb, the driver explains that we're naked because we're dead. No one questions this story. Maybe they're convinced by our fennel, or by our nakedness. Maybe they know that lovers, like the dead, inhabit a country of their own, closed to everybody else. Because we didn't have time to wash after making love, our bodies smell of seawater. As we drive around the island, the driver stops at every beach, and we wash each other. We add more salt to our salt, wetness to our wetness.

Near dawn, when we return to the street outside our hotel, the driver asks if we want to go back to our country. No, we tell him, we've decided to stay a while, and he looks at us strangely. When we leave the cab, he waits. We find a small bar in the basement of a house across from the hotel. The bartender dozes with her head on the bar. A few couples sway on the dance floor. The piano player laces a little Bach into his blues. Yellow blossoms blaze on the fennel you hold over your head.

Chapter 27

Dusk, she wonders, or *twilight*? Which has enough purple to erase these stripes of brown haze blurring the tops of the palms? Which floor is she on? Thirty-three? Thirty-four? She could look at the key to read her room number. It isn't a key, though, just a strip of gray plastic. She misses the weight of an old-fashioned hotel key, the scent of metal in her sweaty hand. She remembers her first hotel key in Paris. That's where she should be now, one story above the street, listening as Algerian voices seep through the thickening light. At midnight a young man under her window will blow one note from a trumpet, a sound shiny as a pear, and as soft. That Paris isn't quite purple, or even lavender, but gray, the grainy color of an old movie. The man in her bed might have had a part in that movie, not a lead, but a bit player who appears in one scene. His face glows, pale even in this light. If she touches his forehead, or his cheek, she'll leave fingerprints, her own irrevocable mark. But she has already touched him. She might be his wife, preparing to lie down with him, or a much younger woman, ready to take his money. She stands on the balcony. A few stars, swollen lights all the way to the dark Pacific. Another dusk, by another ocean— something she read in a book when she was still nearly a girl. She can't remember the author's name, or the title, but she is the character she has forgotten, a woman who walks out of her life, or back in.

–VI–

In Weston's Portrait of Tina

Modotti she raises her arms to pull back her wet hair in her
armpits a little stubble not a full bush nor clean shaven but
those rough beginnings perhaps she is a little careless or busy
or maybe he likes it that way her hair is soaked but she hasn't
just stepped out of the shower her skin glows because the light
caresses tiny beads of sweat on her face and breasts she doesn't
pose for the camera or the photographer but for her lover she
isn't photographed after making love but in the midst of that
act her swollen lips arrested while trembling when this photo
has been taken he will kiss her again the shuddering will
resume his camera records her dark nipples hardened enlarged
because he has bitten there so many times if she tries to speak
no words neither Spanish nor English perhaps a kind of whim-
pering a small mammal in pain hungry thirsty longing a kind
of muteness so like her photographs that typewriter for exam-
ple language waiting for someone to strike

The White Iris

that he should let this trickle of light wash over her face a slow
erosion blurs her mouth a dark blister might be any woman's
sluiced with shadow her collarbone abstract a word in Latin
eyes closed asleep dreaming a car careening on a road in Mexico
or the heat a tropical sweat the scent of an orchid spices the
night if she opens her eyes she won't see him instead that iris
engorged with light swollen an enormous butterfly the corsage
a girl might wear to her first dance this bright slice of her
dream escapes and flies into his lens one piece of her he prints
and holds forever entirely drenched in his glare

The Pleasures of C

i little more than

a child
in profile over
her shoulder
his striped shirt
arm folded
on her breast
a tired wing
her fingers
linger on
her neck's
edge her legs
cross and under
her biceps this
penumbra
of nipple
her naked ear
translucent
on her face
a child's
gravity

ii *The first*

nudes
of C
were amongst
the finest

I had done,
perhaps
the finest.
I did not
wait long
before making
a second
series which
was made on
April 22,
a day
to always
remember.

iii beret

sweater
wristwatch
chair
she straddles
chin on wrists
hard blue eyes
lips a little fuller
more swollen
brow a bit
furrowed
she can take
what he dishes out
she can take

iv *I knew now*

what was coming.
Eyes don't lie
and she wore no mask.

v he records

her transparency
binds her body
to light
sees through
bruise soft
shadow clings
in her cleft
chin stutters
across her
breakable
cheekbones
eyes
the color
of no other

vi *You see*

I really wanted
C
hence my hesitation.

vii everybody remembers

her
as these eggs
pale ovals
elliptical orbits
no eyes
no mouth
no face
the perfect woman
no aperture
except his lens

viii *I am slow*

especially
if I am
deeply moved.
I opened
a bottle
of wine...

ix the city

sliced
by the blind
three-quarters
of the photo
mutilated
impossible
to read
industrial
warehouses over
her bed a lamp
off now
as if later
to dissect
asleep
on her belly
no sheet
to cover
wrists crossed
underwater
light
caresses

x *I made some eighteen*

negatives,
delaying,
always

delaying,
until at last
she lay
below me
waiting,
holding
my eyes
with hers.

xi that she should float

hair spread
a sliver
of soap
dissolves
in this
water
forever
an endless
pool
his salt

xii *And*

I was lost
and have been
lost
ever since.

–VII–

Postcards

Pennsylvania

This quilt sutured
with Amish
stitches by a woman
who begets
in a nightgown
and despises buttons:
that's why
our seasons flare
maple and corn, flagrant
as dusk locks
each window. A train
itches between stars
while everybody rides
tethered to bunks,
scrubbed and damp.

Rome

A blind man drives
his cab in circles
through an empty city.
Our Pope dozes,
untroubled by dreams.
A translation
erases all marble.
Only whitewash
to write on. Fresh
fur, the statue
a woman
wagging
a dog's tail.

Amsterdam

Sky without hills
so many bridges
each one severed
by a piano
playing as it rises
through a third floor window
on that hook
Europe hangs from.

Nevada

A desert
of discarded nickels,
scent of prostate cancer
in the older casinos.
Spin that wheel, baby.
Choississez.
Le rouge, ou le noir?
An old story
mistranslated
one more time.

Montana

In this heat
one letter is plenty,
an M
to stand for a town,
flat in August,
nobody knows the name of.
M.M.,
blond as uranium,
slender as fusion.
I have a photo
of her
in the desert
sucking her thumb.

San Antonio

A river splits
our night
as a skinny
girl runs the wet
edge—
neon pesos,
unburied treasure.

Kentucky

All you know
about blue
grass is
Catherine
the Great
in the horse barns
again. When your X-
wife doesn't cinch
the saddle, red
mud rhymes
your mount.

Sodom

Salt. A residue
of lovers' tears
basting the bottom
of this tin
plain. Lick
and you'll taste
with your longest
tongue,
deer and cows
damp as August.
In another
story, some
body runs
under a rain
you translate
night
after night.

The Southern Cross

What you saw, once,
on an island
above the sweat. Nobody
believes you now, that icy
itch, all those sleepy cars
adrift between stars. Name
your Arabs—Betelgeuse,
Aldebaran—and swim home.

Notes

"Crepusucle with Nellie," "Live at the Five Spot," "Pannonica," "Round Lights": Thelonious Monk.

"Woman Speaking, Street Corner," "John Coltrane, Half Note, 1960": Roy deCarava.

"Blue Room": Edward Hopper.

"Paris": César Vallejo.

"Prostate": Lars Gustaffson, *Webster's New World Dictionary of the American Language.*

"Stain": Carlo Ginzberg.

"Fireworks over Ryōgken Bridge": Hiroshige, John Logan.

"Seventh Age": Osip Mandelstam.

"Our Small Republic": Federico Fellini.

"In Weston's Portrait of": Edward Weston.

"The White Iris": Edward Weston.

"The Pleasures of C": Edward Weston. Italicized passages are quoted from Edward Weston's journals.

PHOTO: Jean Morrison

EDWARD SMALLFIELD'S poems and stories have appeared in *The Battery Review, Fourteen Hills, Manoa, Seven Hundred Kisses, Yellow Silk, ZYZZYVA,* and other periodicals. With Toni Mirosevich and Charlotte Muse, he is the author of *Trio. One Hundred Famous Views of Edo,* a collaboration with Doug MacPherson, will be published by Battery Press this fall.

SMCL

3 5151 00226 3838